America

Come on a journey of discovery

Elaine Jackson

Copyright © QEB Publishing, Inc. 2004

First published in the United States by
QEB Publishing
23062 La Cadena Drive
Laguna Hills
Irvine
CA 92653

This edition published by
Teacher Created Resources, Inc.
6421 Industry Way
Westminster CA 92683

www.teachercreated.com

Library of Congress Control Number 2004101779

ISBN 978 1 4206 8277 9

Written by Elaine Jackson
with additional text by Ruth Urbom
Designed by Starry Dog Books Ltd
Edited by Christine Harvey
Map by PCGraphics (UK) Ltd

Creative Director Louise Morley
Editorial Manager Jean Coppendale

Printed and bound in China

Picture credits
Key: t = top, b = bottom, m = middle, c = centre,
l = left, r = right.

Art Directors & TRIP Eric Smith 6-7 / Adina Tovy
6ml / Picturesque 8-9 / Anne-Marie Bazalik 9tl
/ Viesti Associates 9tr / Bob Turner 14-15 / Adina Tovy
18bl / Tom Campbell 20-21 / Spencer Grant 21br
/ Adina Tovy 24-25 / Spencer Grant 26-27 / Martin
Barlow 26tr / Adina Tovy 27tr **Corbis** Dean Conger
10bl / Mark Peterson 10tl / Annie Griffith 12 / Nathan
Benn 12tl / David Muench 13tr / Philip Gould 15tr
/ Joseph Sohm 15tl / Jim Sugar 18tr / Gunter Marx
19 / John Van Hasselt 20tr / Adam Woolfitt 23tl / Larry
Lee 23bl / Mike Segar 26tl **Getty Images** Paul
Souders 8tr / David Young-Wolf pt l / Gary Holscher
16bl / Arthur Tilley 22.

The words in **bold** can
be found in the Glossary
on page 28.

Contents

KEY

- City ●
- River 〜
- Lake
- Country Border ‑‑‑
- Mountains ▲▲
- Swamp

1 VERMONT
2 NEW HAMPSHIRE
3 MASSACHUSETTS
4 RHODE ISLAND
5 CONNECTICUT
6 NEW JERSEY
7 DELAWARE
8 MARYLAND
9 WEST VIRGINIA

ATLANTIC OCEAN

Boston
New York
Washington DC
Philadelphia

MAINE
ONTARIO
NEW YORK
PENNSYLVANIA
VIRGINIA
NORTH CAROLINA
SOUTH CAROLINA
Appalachian Mountains
GEORGIA
FLORIDA
Everglades

Erie
Huron
MICHIGAN
OHIO
INDIANA
KENTUCKY
TENNESSEE
ALABAMA
New Orleans
Gulf of Mexico

Michigan
Superior
WISCONSIN
ILLINOIS
Mississippi
MISSOURI
ARKANSAS
Mississippi
LOUISIANA

CANADA

Hudson Bay

Minneapolis
MINNESOTA
IOWA
Missouri
NORTH DAKOTA
SOUTH DAKOTA
NEBRASKA
KANSAS
Great Plains
OKLAHOMA
TEXAS

UNITED STATES OF AMERICA

MEXICO

Missouri
MONTANA
Yellowstone National Park
WYOMING
Colorado
COLORADO
NEW MEXICO
IDAHO
UTAH
Grand Canyon
ARIZONA

Rocky Mountains

WASHINGTON
OREGON
NEVADA
Las Vegas
Death Valley
CALIFORNIA
Los Angeles
San Diego
San Francisco

ARCTIC OCEAN

Bering Strait

Mount McKinley
ALASKA (USA)

N E
W S

HAWAII (USA)
Mauna Kea
Mauna Loa
PACIFIC OCEAN

PACIFIC OCEAN

1000 miles
1000 km
0
0

Tropic of Cancer

4

Where in the world is the U.S.?

The United States of America (often called the U.S.) lies on the **continent** of North America. It is bordered on the west by the Pacific Ocean, on the east by the Atlantic Ocean and on the south by the Gulf of Mexico. The country to the north of the U.S. is Canada and to the south is Mexico.

The U.S. is the world's third-largest country (after Russia and Canada). It has the world's third-largest population (after China and India).

▼ The United States of America's place in the world.

the U.S.

▲ The national flag of the U.S., often referred to as the "Stars and Stripes."

Did you know?

Name United States of America
Location North America
Surrounding countries
Canada and Mexico
Surrounding oceans and seas
Atlantic Ocean, Pacific Ocean, Gulf of Mexico
Length of coastline 12,380 miles
Capital city Washington, DC
Area 3,787,276 square miles
Population 301,139,947 (2007 estimate)
Life expectancy Male 72, Female 79
Religions Christian 84% (Protestant 56%, Roman Catholic 28%), Jewish 2%
Languages English, Spanish widely spoken
Climate Mostly **temperate** along the coasts, **tropical** in Hawaii and Florida, **arid** in the southwest, **arctic** in Alaska
Highest mountain Mount McKinley (also called Denali) in Alaska (20,322 feet)
Major rivers Mississippi (length: 2,348 miles), Missouri (length: 2,315 miles), Arkansas (length: 1,459 miles), Colorado (length: 1,450 miles)
Currency U.S. dollar. There are 100 cents in one dollar.

What is the U.S. like?

Traveling across the landscape

The U.S. consists of 50 states. As you travel through the U.S., you will be amazed at the wide variety of landscapes. There are vast mountain ranges, huge flat grassy **plains**, hot deserts, and frozen **glaciers**.

▼ A beach on Kauai, one of the islands of Hawaii.

The southeast

The southern coast along the Gulf of Mexico contains the great **delta** of the Mississippi River. If you travel here, you will see the **swamps** of the Everglades in Florida. This part of the U.S. is hit by hurricanes more than any other part.

Central U.S.

The huge flat area known as the Great Plains is in the center of the U.S. and extends westward to the Rocky Mountains. Almost all the rivers and streams in the central part of the U.S. flow into the Mississippi–Missouri river system.

The west

West of the Great Plains are the snow-capped Rocky Mountains. In the south of this region is the world's deepest valley, the Grand Canyon.

There is a fracture in the Earth's crust, running from San Francisco to Mexico, called the San Andreas Fault. The area around the San Andreas Fault suffers frequent earthquakes.

Alaska and Hawaii

Alaska and Hawaii only became U.S. states in 1959. They are separated from the rest of the USA and have very different climates and landscapes.

Alaska, in the extreme northwest of North America, is an area of dramatic landscapes with glaciers and **fjords**.

Hawaii consists of a group of volcanic islands in the middle of the Pacific Ocean. Mauna Kea and Mauna Loa on the island of Hawaii are active volcanoes; the volcanoes on the other Hawaiian islands are no longer active. Hawaii has a tropical climate.

▲ The Majorie Glacier is situated in Glacier Bay, in Alaska. It sheds huge chunks of ice. This is known as "calving". Boat cruises to see the glacier are very popular.

Did you know?

Death Valley in California has one of the most extreme climates on earth. It has baking heat and burning sands. Badwater Basin in Death Valley is the lowest place in the western hemisphere. It is one of the hottest places in the entire world—temperatures there can reach 113°F!

◀ The Grand Canyon, one of the world's most impressive scenic wonders, is located in the state of Arizona.

Another state, another climate!

▼ Hurricanes and tornadoes can cause massive damage to houses and other buildings.

A varied climate

As you travel around the U.S., you will experience wide variations in the weather. The climate ranges from sizzling temperatures in the California desert to below freezing in Alaska.

The western coastal states

Oregon and Washington in the northwest region along the Pacific coast are among the wettest parts of the country. Temperatures here are mild all year round. Summers in California are generally dry, and inland areas can get very hot.

The central states

The central areas of the U.S. are far away from the oceans, so as a result their climates are more extreme. It can get extremely cold with a lot of snow in the wintertime and then very hot in the summer. The Great Plains can receive heavy rainfall in severe thunderstorms, with dangerous lightning and occasional tornadoes!

The northeast states

If you visit states such as Maine, Massachusetts, and Pennsylvania, you will experience different weather at different times of the year. In winter, these areas have heavy snow and freezing rain. Summers are usually sunny and warm, or even hot.

The southeast states

States such as Florida, Georgia, and South Carolina experience moderate rainfall fairly evenly throughout the year. The winters are quite mild and short. Summers are hot and humid. Southern Florida usually has good weather all year round.

▼ Tornadoes can move quickly across the flat lands of the Great Plains.

▼ The Rocky Mountains receive a lot of snow in winter, so skiing is good.

The southwest states

States such as Arizona and New Mexico have the hottest temperatures in the U.S. Unlike the southeast states, the climate here is very dry.

In January, David is visiting his cousin in Colorado.

❓ What do you think the weather will be like? ❓

❓ What kind of clothes should he pack? ❓

What kinds of outdoor ❓ activities do you think they might do?

Eating across America

Food origins

The food eaten in the U.S. is a mixture of native foods and favorite meals brought to the country by **immigrants**. Recipes that the ancestors of today's Americans brought with them from their homelands are often passed down through families.

Although people all across America eat many of the same foods, there are some that are more popular in certain areas. For example, fresh seafood is a big favorite in coastal areas.

Some types of foods and cooking are popular all across America. Mexican foods such as tacos and tortilla chips

▼American families enjoy going out to eat together.

have been eaten throughout the U.S. for a long time. Chinese and Italian foods are also common in every region.

Eating out

Americans enjoy the convenience of eating in restaurants. Many people who travel to the U.S. are surprised by the huge size of meals served in some American restaurants. But if you are unable to finish all your meal in a family restaurant, you can ask for the leftovers to be put into a "doggie bag" which you can take home with you. You don't have to give it to the dog, though – you can finish the rest of your meal yourself later!

◀ People in New England enjoy eating fresh seafood.

Thanksgiving is on the fourth Thursday of November and dates back to 1621. When the Pilgrims came to America from England, about half of them died in their first winter. They turned to the Native Americans for help, and were taught how to plant crops. The good harvest the next fall inspired the Pilgrims to give thanks by holding a feast. Foods eaten at that first Thanksgiving have become traditional and are still eaten today. Our whole family gets together for Thanksgiving and we have a really special meal. We have roast turkey, corn, sweet potatoes, cranberry sauce, and pumpkin pie.

Amy wrote to her English pen pal about her family's Thanksgiving celebrations in the U.S.

Fast food

Fast-food restaurants that originated in America have spread all over the world. Many Americans like to grab a quick, tasty hamburger, hot dog, or donut as they hurry from place to place in their busy lives.

▼ American families get together to enjoy a big Thanksgiving meal.

The Mississippi River

About the river

The name *Mississippi* comes from a Native American word meaning "great waters." The **source** of the mighty Mississippi is a number of very small streams in northern Minnesota. As the Mississippi flows south, it is joined by many **tributaries** including the Missouri River. The Mississippi forms part of the borders of ten different states.

Finally, the water flows into the Gulf of Mexico and leaves behind the soil it has been carrying along. This soil forms a huge delta. The Mississippi river system is a busy shipping route and it also provides a home for many kinds of wildlife.

▶ Traditional paddlewheel steamboats on the Mississippi River in St. Louis, Missouri.

▲ The Mississippi forms many small channels when it reaches its delta, where it flows into the Gulf of Mexico.

▲ Several small streams form the source of the Mississippi.

Dear Kayla,
We took a steamboat tour along the Mississippi. The scenery was wonderful. Grandpa enjoyed watching the trees and wildlife along the river. The Mississippi is still important for shipping, and we saw lots of big river barges passing by. The Mississippi is the world's third-longest river system, after the Nile and the Amazon.
Love, Grandma and Grandpa

Miss Kayla Jackson
1562 Elm Terrace
Littletown, WA 98001

Kayla's grandparents are on vacation in the southern U.S. They took a tour along the Mississippi in Louisiana on an old-fashioned paddlewheel steamboat. They sent postcards to her, telling her about their trip.

Dear Kayla,
Here in the southern part of the U.S., the Mississippi is at least a mile wide in some places. The water flows slowly toward the Gulf of Mexico. It's hard to believe this huge river starts out in Minnesota as just a small stream! It was so exciting to travel along part of it.
Love, Grandma and Grandpa

Miss Kayla Jackson
1562 Elm Terrace
Littletown, WA 98001

The Great Lakes and Niagara Falls

The Great Lakes

There are five Great Lakes. They are the world's largest group of freshwater lakes. One-fifth of all the fresh water in the world lies in the four upper Great Lakes: Michigan, Huron, Superior and, Erie. Their water is used for drinking and transportation, as a source of power, and for leisure activities.

▼ The natural beauty of Niagara Falls.

Niagara Falls

Water flows from the four upper Great Lakes into the Niagara River. Then, at Niagara Falls, the water plunges 325 feet over a cliff. The sound of Niagara Falls is incredible, as the water spills over and crashes at the bottom. Niagara Falls is the second-largest waterfall in the world. It stretches across the border between the U.S. and Canada. The water then travels 15 miles to the fifth Great Lake—Ontario. From Lake Ontario, the water enters the Saint Lawrence River and continues on to the Atlantic Ocean.

▲ Lake Superior is one of the largest freshwater lakes in the world.

Jason is doing a project on the Great Lakes for homework. He made notes of some facts about each of them.

LAKE SUPERIOR
- largest of the Great Lakes
- deepest and coldest
- surrounded by forests
- Lake Superior is big enough to hold all the water from the other Great Lakes!

LAKE MICHIGAN
- second largest of the Great Lakes
- the only Great Lake entirely within the U.S.
- some large **urban** areas are located on its shores, such as Chicago

LAKE HURON
- third largest of the lakes
- very productive fishing industry
- has over 30,000 islands

LAKE ERIE
- smallest of the Great Lakes
- shallowest of the five Great Lakes, so it warms quickly in the spring and freezes over in winter

LAKE ONTARIO
- similar in size to Lake Erie, but much deeper
- holds almost four times as much water as Lake Erie

Traveling through the farming regions

The U.S. is the world's leading producer of food and provides for almost all its own food needs. It is the world's leading **exporter** of wheat and corn. It is also a major world producer of cheese, soybeans, tobacco, tomatoes, cattle (for beef), chickens, pigs, cotton, and sugar.

▼ Wine is produced in California.

Central USA

As you travel across the Great Plains, you will see large open areas of land with farms and ranches. Huge machines are used to plant and harvest the crops, such as wheat, which are grown in vast fields. Beef cattle are also raised throughout most of the Great Plains. Cattle ranching is especially important in Texas, where real cowboys still ride horses to do their work.

Northern and eastern areas

The area around the Great Lakes is important for **dairy** farming. There are more dairy cows in the state of Wisconsin than in any other U.S. state. Milk, cheese, and other dairy products are produced in this region. New York and Vermont lead in the production of maple syrup.

▼ Fruit trees grow well in the northwest of the country.

The southeast

As you travel on to the southeast, you will see the tobacco-growing areas of North Carolina. Peanuts are produced in Georgia. Florida, with its tropical climate, is America's leading grower of oranges and other citrus fruits.

California

California is America's leading producer of fruit and vegetables, such as lettuce, broccoli, strawberries, and melons. A wide variety of produce is grown in the **fertile** soil of California's huge Central Valley.

California produces some of the world's greatest wines. The area has well-drained soil, warm days, and cool nights, which are good conditions for wine grapes.

The northwest

The cooler climate of this region makes it suitable for growing fruits such as apples, pears, plums, and cherries. The state of Idaho is famous for producing large amounts of potatoes.

▲ The Great Plains are nicknamed the "breadbasket" of the U.S.

Tourism

Visitor attractions

The U.S. has plenty to offer visitors. People travel from all over to lie on sandy beaches and swim in the warm water off Florida's coasts, or to go skiing in the Rocky Mountains. There are historic places to visit, such as Boston in New England or Vicksburg on the Mississippi River, or the big-city excitement and shopping of New York or Los Angeles.

▲ The swampy wetlands of the Florida Everglades attract visitors eager to learn about the plants and wildlife there.

▼ Florida is famous for its theme parks, such as Disney World.

Natural wonders

The U.S. has many natural attractions, including glaciers in Alaska, deserts in the southwest and **geysers** in Wyoming. There are many national parks and forests where people can enjoy watching wild animals in their natural **habitat**. Yellowstone National Park, located in Idaho, Montana and Wyoming is the oldest park in the USA.

Hi Jessica,
I'm having a great time here in Florida. We went to Disney World yesterday, which was fantastic— there was just so much to do! I loved all the rides. We've spent a lot of time at the beach. The sun shines every day—no wonder they call it the Sunshine State!
I just don't want this vacation to end.
See you soon,
Max

Jessica Phillips
604 Maplewood Drive
Pittsburgh, PA 15122

▼ Yellowstone National Park has thousands of hot springs and natural geysers, including the world-famous Old Faithful geyser, which shoots out a jet of water approximately every hour.

Industry and education

More than one type of power

During the 20th century, the U.S. became the richest and most powerful country in the world. It has vast resources, including deposits of iron ore and oil. The country's huge energy needs are met by its natural resources, such as **hydroelectric power**, as well as electricity produced from coal, oil, and nuclear power.

Working in the U.S.

Most people have a very high standard of living. Unemployment is low and highly-educated workers can earn good salaries. About three-quarters of Americans work in service industries, such as **retail**, banking, insurance, healthcare, teaching, and tourism.

Industry

American scientists have a long history of making technological advances in many fields. In 1969, U.S. scientists built the first spaceship to take people to the moon and back. Today, the U.S. leads the world in computer technology and in developing medical, **aerospace**, and military equipment.

▼ The Coca Cola Company is famous throughout the world. There is even a museum in Atlanta dedicated to it.

America's aluminum, steel, and car **industries** are among the biggest in the world. The U.S. exports **raw materials** such as cotton, iron, and chemical products around the world.

Other major industries include publishing, food processing, entertainment, **telecommunications**, and paper.

▼ Hydroelectric power is provided by the Hoover Dam on the border between Arizona and Nevada.

Education

Children enter kindergarten, the first year of school, at age 5. Each fall they begin a new grade. Elementary school usually consists of kindergarten through grade six, and children stay until about the age of 12. Secondary education is usually divided into junior high school (grades 7–9) and senior high school (grades 10–12). After graduating from high school, over 60 percent of students continue their education at a college or university. There are over 3,000 universities and colleges in the U.S.

▼ U.S. scientists conduct important new research.

The nation's capital

▶ The US President lives and works in the White House.

Washington, DC is America's capital city. The letters DC stand for "District of Columbia," which is the official title for the area where the city of Washington is located. It is not actually located within any of the 50 U.S. states. When Washington was chosen to become the national capital, it was thought that it would be unfair if any one state received the honor of being the location of the national government.

Washington, DC is named after George Washington, who was the first President of the U.S. Before he was elected to be the first President, George Washington was famous as an army general in the Revolutionary War, when the U.S. won its independence from Great Britain.

The seat of government

The President and Vice-President live and work in Washington. The President lives in the White House, which also contains his office (known as the Oval Office because of its shape) as well as offices for his staff.

The U.S. Congress, America's national law-making organization, meets in the U.S. Capitol Building in Washington.

There are two houses of Congress to which members are elected: the Senate and the House of Representatives.

The highest court, the U.S. Supreme Court, and many other government departments are also located in Washington.

◀ The U.S. Capitol Building houses the offices and meeting chambers of the Senate and the House of Representatives.

▶ The Lincoln Memorial in Washington, DC honors President Abraham Lincoln, who is remembered for freeing the slaves in the 1860s.

Did you know?

In Washington's many museums you can see important objects from significant historical events. For example, at the National Air and Space Museum you can see the plane that made the world's first successful flight in 1903, as well as part of the spacecraft that carried the first astronauts to walk on the moon in 1969.

Amazing, but true!

When it was built in 1800, the White House was the largest house in the entire country.

In 1814, the White House and the Capitol Building were partially burned down by British soldiers.

The White House has its own swimming pool, bowling alley, and movie theater for the President and his family.

New York, New York!

▶ The Statue of Liberty is America's symbol of freedom.

Where is New York?

There are actually two places called New York: New York City and New York State. New York City, or the "Big Apple" as it is sometimes called, lies at the mouth of the Hudson River. Even though New York City is by far the largest city in New York State, it is not the state capital. The state government is located in the capital city of Albany.

Manhattan

The first Europeans to settle on Manhattan Island in the 1620s were the Dutch. They called the city New Amsterdam. In 1664, the British took over and renamed it New York. Manhattan is now one of the five boroughs at the heart of this huge city.

A multicultural city

Since the early days of the U.S., New York has been a place where people from all over the world have come to start new lives in America. As a result, most of the languages of the world are spoken by New York's multicultural inhabitants.

◀ The New York Knicks are a popular basketball team. They play in orange, blue and white - the official colors of New York City.

Josh decided to write an article about New York City for his class travel brochure.

▼ New York has many huge skyscrapers.

A visit to the observation room on the 86th floor of the Empire State Building will allow you to see breathtaking views over New York.

After this, take a trip on the Staten Island Ferry to see the Statue of Liberty. Then move on to the hustle and bustle of Times Square. Broadway and 42nd Street, famous for their theaters and restaurants, meet here. The city also has lots of museums and great shopping streets.

If, after all this excitement, you are finding the streets hot and stuffy, Central Park offers the biggest green space in the city. Here you can stroll through the park or take part in activities such as pony riding, tennis, or skating.

Traveling to California and the west coast cities

About California

California is the third-largest state in the U.S. Its nickname is the "Golden State." In 1849, thousands of people rushed to California in search of gold after it was discovered there. Today, California has the largest population of any state in the U.S.

▶ In San Francisco, cable cars rattle around the city's hilly streets.

SAN FRANCISCO
This is one of America's most unusual cities. San Francisco has a wonderful harbor and bay. It has famous bridges, such as the Golden Gate Bridge. The San Francisco area sometimes has earthquakes, so buildings are built to be "earthquake proof."

By Katie

Josh's friends decided to find out about the cities on the west coast for their class travel brochure.

HOLLYW

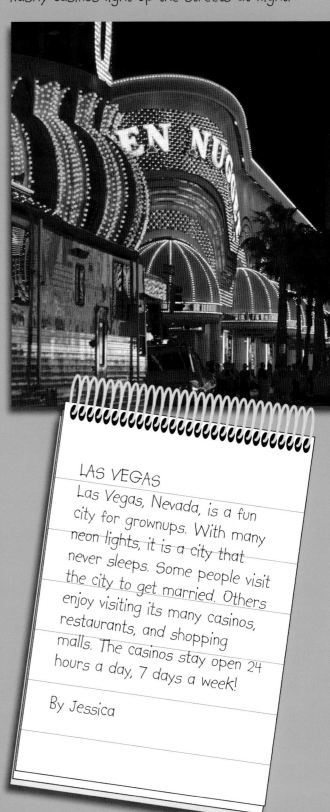

▼ Las Vegas is in the Nevada desert. The flashy casinos light up the streets at night.

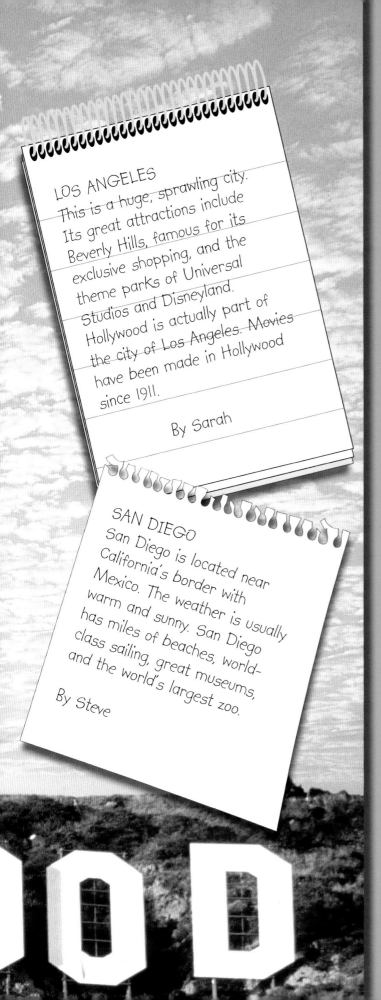

LOS ANGELES
This is a huge, sprawling city. Its great attractions include Beverly Hills, famous for its exclusive shopping, and the theme parks of Universal Studios and Disneyland. Hollywood is actually part of the city of Los Angeles. Movies have been made in Hollywood since 1911.

By Sarah

SAN DIEGO
San Diego is located near California's border with Mexico. The weather is usually warm and sunny. San Diego has miles of beaches, world-class sailing, great museums, and the world's largest zoo.

By Steve

LAS VEGAS
Las Vegas, Nevada, is a fun city for grownups. With many neon lights, it is a city that never sleeps. Some people visit the city to get married. Others enjoy visiting its many casinos, restaurants, and shopping malls. The casinos stay open 24 hours a day, 7 days a week!

By Jessica

◀ Hollywood is the center of America's film industry.

Glossary

aerospace
companies involved in building airplanes and spacecraft

arctic
an arctic climate is very cold, with a lot of snow

arid
very dry, with almost no rain

continent
one of the seven large areas of land on the Earth's surface: Africa, Asia, Australia, Antarctica, North America, South America, and Europe

dairy
a place where cows' milk is taken and made into other food products

delta
an area at the mouth of a large river where the river flows into the ocean

exports
goods sold to other countries

fertile
able to grow or produce a lot of things

fiord
a narrow area of sea that has tall rocky cliffs along its sides

geyser
a natural hot spring which shoots a jet of hot water into the air

glacier
a huge mass of ice that moves slowly across the land

habitat
a natural area where animals live

hydroelectric power
electricity made from the controlled flow of water

immigrants
people who have come to live in a new country

industry
the business of making things in factories or workshops

plain
a large area of low, flat land

raw materials
things such as iron or coal that are used for making other goods

retail
selling things in stores

source
where a river or stream starts

swamp
an area of low-lying land which is permanently wet

telecommunications
telephones and the wires and networks for connecting them

temperate
a temperate climate is not too hot or too cold

tributary
a river or stream that flows into another, often larger, one

tropical
a tropical climate is hot and rainy

urban
located in a large town or city

Index

Teaching ideas and activities for children

The **Travel Through** series offers up-to-date information and interdisciplinery knowledge in subject areas such as geography, language arts, mathematics, history, and social studies. The series enables children to develop an overview ("the big picture") of each country. This overview reflects the huge diversity and richness of the life and culture of each country. The series aims to prevent the development of misconceptions, stereotypes, and prejudices, which often develop when the focus of a study narrows too quickly onto a small locality within a country. The books will help children gain access to this overview, and also develop an understanding of the interconnectedness of places. They contribute to children's geographical knowledge, skills, and understanding, and help them to make sense of the world around them.

The following activities promote thinking skills and creativity. The activities in section A are designed to help children develop critical thinking skills, while the activities in section B are designed to promote different types of learning styles.

A: ACTIVITIES TO DEVELOP THINKING SKILLS
ACTIVITIES TO PROMOTE RESEARCH AND RECALL OF FACTS
Ask the children to:
• make an alphabet book for a young child, illustrating the contrasts in the U.S. (for example, physical features, weather, industry).
• research and investigate a mountain environment (the Rocky Mountains) or a tropical swamp area (the Florida Everglades). The children could present their information in a poster or a Powerpoint presentation.

ACTIVITIES TO PROMOTE UNDERSTANDING

Ask the children to:

• replicate a simple map or picture of the U.S. Place the children in groups of four to six. Tell them they are going to reproduce the map or picture you have provided. In their groups, ask them to number themselves and to discuss strategies they could use to reproduce your picture. Call each number, one at a time, to look at the picture for two minutes. Then ask them to go back and draw what they can remember, while discussing the picture and strategies with their group. Give the children five minutes to do this. Then call the next member of the group, and so on. At the end, show the children the original and ask them to evaluate each group's work.

• make a flow chart to show "A year in the life of a cotton plant" or "The production of corn."

ACTIVITIES TO PROMOTE THE USE OF KNOWLEDGE AND SKILLS TO SOLVE PROBLEMS

Ask the children to:

• make notes to explain the reasons why the streets in New York are so busy and there are so many traffic jams.

• produce a poster, in groups, advertising different types of vacations around the U.S.

ACTIVITIES TO ENCOURAGE ANALYTICAL THINKING

Ask the children to:

• compare and contrast life in New York with a small city or town.

• use reference books and the Internet to write a journalistic report about an earthquake in California or a tornado in the Great Plains.

ACTIVITIES TO PROMOTE CREATIVITY

Ask the children to:

• make a representation of the Florida Everglades or the Grand Canyon, using collage or painting.

• design a word search, including geographical words.

ACTIVITIES TO HELP CHILDREN USE EVIDENCE TO FORM OPINIONS AND EVALUATE CONSEQUENCES OF DECISIONS

Ask the children to:

• rank five of the places in this book in order of preference, giving reasons why they would like to visit them.

• in pairs, decide on five items that would best represent life in the U.S.

B: ACTIVITIES BASED ON DIFFERENT LEARNING STYLES

ACTIVITIES FOR LINGUISTIC LEARNERS

Ask the children to:

• write a rap to promote New York as a great place for a vacation.

• write a journalistic report about living in the "Big Apple."

ACTIVITIES FOR LOGICAL AND MATHEMATICAL LEARNERS

Ask the children to use the Internet to find out about the climate in Florida and Alaska, and to represent the differences graphically.

ACTIVITIES FOR VISUAL LEARNERS

Ask the children to:

• locate the major cities and rivers on a map of the U.S.

• draw their favorite place in the U.S. on a postcard-sized piece of cardboard.

ACTIVITIES FOR KINESTHETIC LEARNERS

Ask the children to:

• make some hamburgers (with adult support).

• make a model of a volcanic eruption on Mauna Loa or Mauna Kea.

• enact the eruption of a volcano, using dance and drama. Some children can be the core, others the mantle, melted rock, and the crust.

ACTIVITIES FOR MUSICAL LEARNERS

Ask the children to create and perform a simple country music tune, using available instruments.

ACTIVITIES FOR INTER-PERSONAL LEARNERS

Ask the children to plan an itinerary for a two-week vacation for their family.

ACTIVITIES FOR INTRA-PERSONAL LEARNERS

Ask the children to describe how they would feel looking across New York from the 102nd floor of the Empire State Building, or flying over the Grand Canyon in a helicopter.

ACTIVITIES FOR NATURALISTIC LEARNERS

Ask the children to make notes and prepare a speech for a debate on either the pros or the cons of maintaining the national parks and/or wilderness areas in the U.S.